101 THINGS EVERY
KID NEEDS TO KNOW

Important Skills That Prepare Kids for Life!

JAMIE THORNE

ISBN: 978-1-962481-02-1

FREE BONUS

SCAN TO GET OUR NEXT
BOOK FOR FREE!

Table of Contents

GROWING AS A
SELF-RELIANT
INDIVIDUAL

[1]
COOKING SIMPLE RECIPES

Cooking is an essential life skill that allows you to turn separate ingredients into something delicious. The act of cooking not only encourages you to use your creativity, but it can also boost your confidence and foster a sense of independence.

Before getting started, it's important to always make sure there's adult supervision when you're using a stovetop, oven, knives, or other potentially dangerous utensils. Ideally, an adult should provide clear instructions, demonstrate proper cooking techniques, and oversee the entire process. Don't try cooking alone unless your parents, guardians, or caregivers have told you that you can!

Step one is to choose an age-appropriate recipe that utilizes ingredients you enjoy. Choose recipes that use only basic techniques like mixing, measuring, and stirring rather than complex cooking methods that may ask for grating, peeling, and chopping.

Step two is to wash your hands before and after handling food. You'll need to put the ingredients out on the countertop so that they're easy to reach when needed. You should also know what utensils you'll need and gather them. This can include things like bowls, measuring cups, oven mitts, pot holders, cutting boards, and knives.

Step three is to prepare your meal by following the recipe. Don't skip ahead, as each step is important. For example, you shouldn't skip the step that says to let instant macaroni and cheese sit for 90 seconds on the countertop after it's heated. This step allows the cheese to become firmer and less watery.

By preparing a simple yet delicious meal, you'll be able to feed yourself safely and gain valuable independence.

[2]
SAFELY USE STOVE AND KITCHEN UTENSILS

The kitchen is full of useful tools, but some of them can be dangerous if you don't know how to use them. It's important to understand potential hazards and what to do if you hurt yourself. Make sure an adult shows you how to program the oven, set a timer, and use utensils without causing harm to yourself or others.

Each stove has knobs and buttons on it. These will turn on the stove or oven and allow you to set a timer. When the timer goes off after 30 minutes, for example, that does not mean that the burners or oven automatically turn off. This just means that the time your food needs to cook has been reached. Always turn off every knob and button when you're done cooking.

Look at your recipe to know how hot the stove or oven should be. Some recipes will call for a low heat, while others will call for a higher temperature. Knobs may turn from a level 1 to a level 5, with the higher numbers representing hotter temperatures.

Make sure you turn on the correct knob. Each one is connected to a different part of the stove. It's also important to avoid placing an empty pot or pan on a burner. This can create smoke and trigger a fire alarm. Most recipes start with a liquid first, such as oil or water, followed by ingredients like spices and vegetables.

Avoid using sharp utensils that are too big for your hand. If the handle feels like you can't grab it well, use a smaller knife. Be sure to clean the pots and pans after you are done cooking, and they're no longer hot. A clean kitchen will keep bugs away and allow your cooking experience to be more enjoyable.

[3]
SEW BY HAND
OR MACHINE

Sewing by hand is a useful skill to learn, especially as you become more independent. A few of the items you'll need include a straight sewing needle, thread, scissors, and fabric. However, make sure the fabric isn't too thick because you need to be able to easily push the needle through the material by hand.

Get double the amount of thread that you think you'll need. If you're sewing a side seam in your shirt (a seam is the place where two pieces of fabric are attached), then you'll need thread that's twice as long as the place that needs to be sewn.

Start out by cutting your thread and pushing one end through the hole in the needle. Next, pull the thread through until the two ends are the same length and can be held together. Tie a knot at the end. Push the needle into one end of the tear in your clothing and pull it all the way through until the knot on the end touches the fabric. Move the needle over a small amount and push it through until it goes out the other side of the fabric. Repeat this until you reach the end of the tear. Finally, cut the thread and tie a knot.

Tips:

- The hole in the needle is called the *eye*.
- Create your own straight seam by placing your fabric pieces on top of each other on a flat surface like a table.
- After you knot your thread, cut the ends, or *tails*, very close to the knot to prevent them from sticking up.
- You don't want your stitches (the thread that goes in and out of the fabric) to show on the outside of the fabric, so turn your clothing inside out to make sure it isn't visible.

[4]
DOING
LAUNDRY

When it comes to cleaning your clothes in a washing machine, the first thing to know is which colors you can and can't wash together. White, pale pinks, pale blues, tans, and cream-colored items can be washed together. Any other darker color must be washed in a separate load. This is because darker dye can come out in the water in the washing machine and stain lighter-colored clothing.

Read the instructions or ask an adult how much laundry detergent you need to use based on the size of your load. Keep in mind that the more clothes you put in the washing machine, the more water and soap will be needed. You'll also need to know what wash cycle to use, whether that's quick wash, normal, or delicate.

Next, you need to know what temperature the machine should be set. This can be either cool, warm, or hot. Usually, darker-colored items will be washed in cold water, but sometimes people wash everything on the cold setting in separate loads.

Finally, close the door or lid to the washing machine after you've put your clothes and laundry detergent inside. Turn the knobs to the correct settings and press the start button. Don't open the door or lid after the washing cycle has started.

Once the washing cycle is finished, you can put the clothes in the dryer or hang them to dry, whichever way you prefer. After they are dry, fold them and put them away.

[5]
WASHING
DISHES

Whether your home has a dishwasher or you need to wash dishes by hand in the sink, learning how to wash dishes is a valuable skill

If you're going to use a dishwasher, find out if you need to rinse sauces and pieces of food off first. If you do, run water over your cups, plates, bowls, and forks, and then place each one carefully in the dishwasher. Your guardians may have a specific way they want the dishwasher to be filled, so be sure to follow their preferences.

Next, pour the correct amount of detergent into the dispenser or use a pod. Press the button to start the dishwashing cycle. Once the dishes are done, and they aren't too hot from the heated dry feature, you can put the dishes away.

If you're washing dishes by hand, you'll need to run warm water over each dish and wipe off the food and sauce with a sponge that has soap on it. Then rinse off the dish or utensil and place it on a drying rack. Once they're dry, you can put them away.

Tips:

- Don't put pots or pans in the dishwasher unless you're told.
- Don't put sharp knives in the dishwasher without asking if you should and where they need to be placed.
- Dry glass cups right away if washing by hand to avoid water spots.
- Take your time with fragile items, and ask how they need to be washed.
- Be sure to dry off countertops and floors when you're done. Washing dishes can be messy sometimes.

[6]
SWEEPING
AND MOPPING

Keeping the floors of your home clean is a vital life skill. They're constantly being walked on every single day, so it's important to keep your carpeted, tiled, or wooden floors clean and free of germs.

Using a vacuum cleaner is the best way to clean a carpet. You'll need to plug it into a wall outlet and then turn it on. Use long motions as you push and pull the vacuum cleaner across the floors, and make sure to turn it off before unplugging it from the wall.

If you're cleaning a hardwood or tiled floor, you can use a broom or a cloth-bottomed version of a broom to remove dust and crumbs. However, it's important to also mop the floor afterward to remove the germs you can't see.

When you're using a broom, start in one corner of the room and sweep around, pushing the dirt into the same corner until you have a pile. Then go back and do it one more time to pick up smaller pieces you may have missed. Push the dirt and trash into a dustpan and then throw the debris away into the garbage can.

Next, take the mopping bucket and fill it with warm water and the correct amount of soap. Dunk the fabric end of the mop into the warm water until it's soaked. Pull it out and follow the corner-to-corner method you used while sweeping to get the whole floor clean. Be sure to work toward a door so that you can get out of the room after you're done without walking on the wet and clean floors. Empty the dirty water from the bucket and put that and the mop away.

[7]
GROWING PLANTS
AND SEEDS

Planting seeds and watching them grow into vegetables is exciting. You can grow vegetables outside in a garden, inside in planters near a window, or by using a hydroponic system that uses water instead of soil to grow plants. First, you'll need to know what type of vegetable you want to grow. If you're growing more than one type, the time of year when they should be planted and the number of weeks until you can eat them will be different.

Once you know what you want to grow, you need to know how many hours a day of sunshine they should receive and how often you need to water them. For example, if you read that the optimal growing conditions for a certain vegetable is only six hours of sunshine a day, you'll want to find a spot with some shade outside so that they don't receive too much sun.

Next, you need to prepare the soil by taking a garden tool that looks like a huge fork and breaking up any large clumps of dirt. Then you can place one seed at a time in a line down the dirt. Cover each seed with more dirt. If you're using an indoor hydroponic unit, place three seeds into each foam basket and submerge in water.

Be consistent in watering the seeds you put in the soil, and pay attention to whether your window planters are getting enough sun. If not, move them to a window that has more recurring daylight to make sure the seeds will sprout.

After eight or so weeks, many vegetables will be fully grown. Some will be above ground, but others will be mostly in the dirt. Carefully pick your vegetables from the vine or dig in the dirt to harvest them. Clean thoroughly before cooking and eating.

[8]
FIXING OR ASSEMBLING BASIC ITEMS

Knowing how to take care of basic tasks in the home, such as assembling a small table, hanging a picture, or twisting wire on the back of a frame, are all valuable skills to have. However, it's important to know how to use the various tools that are required to do these things. A screwdriver, hammer, pliers, and measuring tape are just some examples. Each serves a specific purpose.

A screwdriver is a tool used to push a screw into something solid, like a wall or piece of wood. Most screwdrivers are manual, meaning you have to turn the tool yourself. However, newer screwdrivers are automatic and have a small motor where the tool twists itself while you hold the handle.

If you're using a screwdriver, turning the handle to the right will push the screw into the wall or wood, while turning it to the left will remove the screw. Avoid removing a screw after you have inserted it into the wall or wood.

A hammer has a heavy metal head that you can use to push a straight nail into a wall or a piece of wood. Make sure that you're using the right size nail as they vary in size. Talk to your parents or guardians and have them help you.

If you're trying to get a nail out of something, you can use pliers, which is a tool used to grab onto small things and pull them out. Sometimes, pliers have sharp blades near the handles. This can be used to cut wire or other similar items. Keep your fingers far away from this blade.

A measuring tape lets you know how far a picture is from the floor or how long a piece of wood is.

Regardless of the tool you're using, you should always wear work gloves and goggles for safety. Be sure to follow assembly instructions and have all the parts and pieces ready to go before you start. Clean up your mess afterward with care, as splinters can hurt!

[9]
DOING HOMEWORK INDEPENDENTLY

Doing your homework on your own will not only help you develop critical thinking skills, but it will also foster good habits. This level of self-reliance will be needed as you enter high school, college, and, eventually, your job.

The first thing you need to do is to decide when and where you can do your homework without distractions. It might be right after school or just before dinner. Maybe it's in the kitchen, on the counter, or in the living room. Try a few places until you find the one that works for you.

Next, organize the tasks you must do and start with the hardest or longest one. Getting this one out of the way while your mind is still fresh is a great habit to form.

Once you sit down to start your homework, set a timer on your phone for 30 minutes (or whatever time works for you). Don't allow yourself to get distracted by your phone or talk to anyone else until the timer rings. Set the timer for three to five minutes and take a short break. Get right back to your homework once the timer goes off, and try to finish it up.

If the tasks are hard and you need a lot of help, set them aside and finish tasks you can complete on your own. Then ask for help once you've completed everything you know how to do.

Try to get the answers yourself before asking for help. Oftentimes, you'll be able to figure out the question after looking at your notes or textbooks. Learning how to quickly find the information you need is vital to your success! This skill can be self-taught and will help you as an adult one day.

[10]
MANAGING
YOUR TIME

You might feel as if you don't have much control over how your daily schedule is planned or unfolds, but you might be able to talk to your loved ones to get ideas for how to make the most out of your day. You might be wondering what it means to use your day fully. For most people, this means that each part of your day has a purpose or meaning to it, so you don't feel bored or lonely.

Let's take a look at the time you have each day outside of school and sports. This way, you can feel like each day is exciting and full of things that keep you busy and entertained.

Take a moment to write down the top five things you like to do around the house. This could include hobbies or other activities. Try to list things that you can do without friends. That way, you can do these activities no matter what else is going on around you.

Next, take a guess at how long you would enjoy doing each of your top five things. Some of them may feel boring after one hour, but others might be fun for many hours.

Finally, write down three things you can do that are good for you but might not be your favorite. This could be something like reading instead of playing video games or practicing guitar instead of listening to music. Try to include these healthy habits when planning your day.

[11]
TAKING ON
NEW CHALLENGES

Trying new things can feel exciting at first. You know that joining a baseball league after school or on Saturdays would be so much fun. But when you show up, you realize that it's very different than throwing the ball around with your friends. It requires work and focus as part of a team. How can you make sure you're facing this challenge and overcoming it? One step at a time.

First, promise yourself that you'll do your best to learn every rule and practice each skill your coach says that you need. Be willing to take corrective criticism even in front of other kids. It's okay to make a mistake when you're new, but try to learn from others. Schedule time to practice without any interruptions.

Don't be hard on yourself or let bad thoughts tear you down. Those thoughts will only hurt you. Instead, think about how excited you are to learn and get better. Track your progress privately, and be sure to praise yourself when you improve.

Relying on others for praise can be risky, especially if they don't praise you often enough or the way you expect. It's better to be your own cheering fan and celebrate the great things you're doing. Challenges will present themselves to you at school, with friends, with siblings, or with other family members. Getting through hard times is a good skill to learn.

GETTING ALONG
WITH OTHERS

[12]
GETTING ALONG WITH SIBLINGS, CLASSMATES, OR TEAMMATES

Each human being is special and different from each other. You may share the same family, class, or team, but you're still your own person with separate interests. Chances are, you like different sports, movies, and hobbies. You probably think different types of jokes are funny, and you have different energy levels. Because of this, it's normal to have tension when you're stuck together. However, there are steps you can take to get along.

One common reason you might have disagreements or bicker is that you both want the same thing. Maybe you and a sibling want to watch television at the same time, or maybe you want to play goalie during the same game as a teammate. The best way to handle this is pretty simple: compromise.

Be willing to watch a movie you don't like because it's not your turn to choose. You might have to wait one more game before you can play goalie. Recognize that other people have wants and needs as well. Being nice sets an example for them to be nice back to you.

If you get into an argument, don't yell or say things you don't mean. It won't make you feel better in the long run. Instead, listen to the other person. They probably have their own view of how the situation should be. Listening can help you reach a solution that's partly what you want and partly what they want. This is an essential part of conflict resolution and negotiation. You can't always control who ends up around you, but you can choose to treat them nicely.

[13]
APPRECIATING TIME WITH OLDER GENERATIONS

There are times when it feels like people from older generations have little in common with you. Whether it's your grandparent or an elderly member of your community, they may not like the same things you like or want to talk about any of the things that are most relevant to your life. How can you respectfully engage with older people and still stay true to who you are?

First, remember that older generations are part of a different time. It would probably be very strange if they were into the video games you love or followed young and trendy influencers. Even though you'll always like different things than they do, this is okay and normal. Ask questions to understand the things they care about.

Once you find something you have in common, even if it's as general as summertime or the beach, then start to talk about that topic. It's okay if you don't like doing the same things at the beach either. You may want to talk about how you love swimming, while they might enjoy reading under an umbrella. Let them tell you about their experience, and you can share yours.

The main attitude you can show is one of interest in their lives, letting them be who they are while you are who you are. If you start to feel bored, you can wait for an opening and change the topic to find something new you both enjoy. Ultimately, it will also make you happy too, especially when you're older and have built memories with grandparents, neighbors, or other elderly loved ones.

[14]
LEARNING SKILLS
FROM PARENTS
OR GUARDIANS

You may sometimes look at your parents or guardians and be really impressed by the variety of cool things they can do! On the other hand, you may feel like you don't have much in common with them, or you may not understand why they do the things that they do. If your mom is always baking or if she loves renovating furniture, but you don't like to do either, then you might also assume there's nothing else she can teach you. But that isn't really true. The skills she has can help you in the future, even if you don't share the same core interests or hobbies.

If you want to learn from your caregivers, the best way to start is by asking them to help you with useful life skills. These can include making basic repairs around the house, doing laundry, planning your finances, or knowing how to cook. All of these are useful things your parents or another trusted adult can teach you.

Typically, adults have a specialty or a set of skills that they're really good at doing. It could be that your parent loves to can fruit or make jams, or maybe they know a lot about a particular time in history.

If you see a loved one doing something interesting, try asking them what they're doing and if they can show you how or explain why they're doing it. For example, you may not think that changing the oil in a car is very interesting right now, but one day that skill can be useful to you when you begin driving your own vehicle. Similarly, you may not think that measuring the height and width of a painting before hanging it on the wall is fun, but knowing how to use a measuring or leveling device is a handy skill to have.

[15]
BEING RESPONSIBLE
FOR YOUR ACTIONS

One thing adults have had to learn during their lives is how to take ownership of what they do and say. Taking responsibility means that you're willing to admit what you said or did regardless of how others react. Starting to do this now will help you learn the impact or effect that each choice you make has on yourself, on others, and on the environment around you.

For example, if you forget to lock the back door at night, that decision could put your household at risk. If someone discovers that you forgot to lock the door, it's important not to lie about it but to own up to that mistake and let everyone know you forgot.

On the flip side, if you remember to lock the door every night for a week, you probably don't need to let everyone know you're doing well with that responsibility. This is true not only at home but also at school. You may answer every quiz or test question correctly, but you can gain a lot of confidence by owning up to areas you're having a hard time with. Knowing your strengths and weaknesses will be a lifelong journey, but it can start now as you figure out what you are really good at and where you may need some help.

Remember that it's okay to ask for help. If you have a new responsibility that you're struggling with, you can ask for support or admit that it might be too much right now. Owning your limitations is a mature skill you'll need at all stages of life.

[16]
BEING PATIENT WITH PEOPLE YOU LIVE WITH

Being patient means that you can sit with discomfort for a long time or wait your turn without trying to rush other people. For example, if you really want to eat dessert but your mom says you need to wait for everyone to finish dinner; first, you may feel like getting up and eating dessert anyway. By waiting your turn, even when it's hard to do, you are showing patience.

Your parents, siblings, caregivers, or other relatives may have different ways of doing ordinary things. Many of their habits might be irritating to you or take too long for your preferences. Unfortunately, this will also be the case when you're an adult at work, in college with a roommate, or at home with your own spouse and kids!

Taking the time to learn how to be patient now will set you up for later success. Being patient is one of many ways you can show that you care and respect other people. You may not even realize how often your loved ones are patient with you too.

For example, you might take too long to get ready to leave the house, but if they don't complain and wait for you quietly, that's their own way of showing patience toward you. It's a valuable gift that can bring you closer to the people who love you and will be there for you. You may disagree with them, but you can still show them you care by waiting and giving them a little extra time or space.

[17]
ENJOYING OUTINGS
WITH LOVED ONES

Sometimes, outings with other people can feel boring or even overwhelming. But in the best of times, outings with your loved ones can create lasting memories and give you a chance to understand them on a deeper level. Imagine you're going to a zoo and you don't like walking around outside, but your brother or sister does. You can take the chance to ask them why they like it. Ask them what animals they enjoy seeing, and maybe discover one or two you enjoy as well.

You might not like going to shopping malls because it takes too long, and you think buying clothes is boring. You can help others by not complaining and trying to be helpful. This way, you won't ruin the experience for others, and the trip will also be finished faster than if you were slowing things down. Even as adults, we must do things that are hard, overwhelming, or boring. Trying to work with your family as a team rather than fight against them will help everyone. You may even learn you like something new along the way.

On the other hand, if you're very excited to go to the zoo or the mall, but you notice it's causing others stress, take the chance to ask them how they're feeling. Maybe you can help them learn to enjoy something you like and encourage them to feel happier. When one person on a joint outing is having a rough time, it can bring down the fun for the rest of the group. Try to be kind to others to make shared experiences as enjoyable as possible for all.

[18]
PROTECTING YOURSELF
AND FAMILY

It's important to know how to handle emergencies. No one wants something scary to happen, but knowing what to do in a scary situation can help keep you safe. If you're home, whether with an adult or by yourself, remember these steps that you can take to be as safe as possible.

First, stay calm. In this situation, staying calm means staying silent. Don't jump, run, yell, or cry because you want to stay as far away from the stranger as possible. You don't want them to know who you are, where you are, or that you're even in the house.

Unless you smell smoke from a fire, be sure to hide immediately in the room you're in when a stranger comes inside. This can be behind a couch, in a closet, or behind a shower curtain. You'll probably want to run into your bedroom or find your parent or caregiver, but that could alert the person of where you are. The exception to this is if you are right next to a back door. If possible, you should run outside and to a trusted neighbor. Otherwise, look around the room you're in and hide.

If you have a phone, turn it to silent once you're hiding. Call 911. If the stranger walks into the room while you're talking to the 911 operator and they see you, don't hang up the phone. You want 911 to hear everything the stranger says to you. This is a scary moment, and you may hear loud or angry noises in your house as you're hiding, but it's important to make sure help is on the way as quickly as possible.

THRIVING IN
SOCIAL SITUATIONS

[19]
MAKE PROPER
EYE CONTACT

Have you ever heard someone call your name only to turn around, and it's your teacher or your uncle whose jokes are cheesy but never funny? You probably don't want to stand and talk to them for a long time, but you know you must show them respect. Your first instinct may be to look away from them, but breaking eye contact may just show that you're shy. It doesn't usually work to end a conversation. Instead of doing that to end a conversation, try practicing good eye contact and using your words to signal you're done.

Good eye contact will tell the world around you that you're confident and friendly. This simply involves looking the other person in their eyes while they're speaking to you and while you're speaking to them. It doesn't mean staring at them without ever looking away. It's okay to take a break and glance away, but for most of the conversation, you should be looking them in their eyes.

This might feel weird at first, but it's a useful skill to build. You'll come across as more trustworthy and polite no matter who you're speaking with or how young or old they are. Take a moment to notice how you feel when people look you in the eye compared to looking at their feet or constantly looking away. Work hard to build this skill, and do your best to consistently practice good eye contact.

[20]
ACTING WITH
MANNERS

By now, you've probably had an adult talk to you about manners. Most people are taught manners because it's important to show respect and consideration to others. Universal codes of behavior help people give and receive a certain level of respect. The first set of manners is to say please and thank you when you ask for and receive something.

Instead of saying, "Can I have a piece of pie?" it would be considered good manners to add the word "please" to your question. If someone gives you something, you should say, "Thank you." Another example of good manners is to know when to say you're sorry. This could be to your friends, siblings, and other people you know. If you've hurt or offended them, saying you're sorry is considered a good step to take to make things right again.

If you want something from your sister's room, or if you want to go outside and play, it's polite to ask permission first. It's rude to just walk into a sibling's room and take something that belongs to them without asking first. It's also inconsiderate to go outside without asking your guardians or parents first, even if you know the answer is going to be yes. Asking first lets them know where you are and shows them that you're aware of safety.

Imagine if someone came into your garage and just took your bike without asking. Then they told you it was okay because they were going to give it back, and you weren't using it right at that moment. You'd be very upset! Other people feel that way, too, when you make decisions about them and their belongings without asking first.

[21]
SHAKING
HANDS

You may have seen adults in your life or on TV shaking hands with someone they've just met. This is a normal and easy thing to do when you meet someone for the first time.

Simply reach out and open your hand, keeping your fingers together. You want to make sure you're holding onto the palm of the other person's hand instead of just squeezing their fingers. It's a good idea to shake their hand up and down about two times.

This may feel a little awkward at first, but that's okay. You might even think it's a weird thing to do with a complete stranger. However, by the time you're an adult, you'll have done the handshaking ritual so many times that you won't even think twice about it.

Usually, when someone is introducing themselves to you, they will also extend their hand for a handshake. Sometimes, older people may even put their free hand on top of your clasped hands. This is meant to show kindness and make you feel at ease. Once the introductions and conversations are over, many people will simply walk away and wave goodbye, but some people will shake hands again. Remember that the handshake in a social setting is optional and not necessary to initiate, but you must return a handshake that is offered to avoid being rude.

[22]
APOLOGIZING
WHEN NECESSARY

There will be times when you hurt someone's feelings or do something that makes them sad or angry. When this happens, and you know you're in the wrong, it's a good idea to offer an apology. An apology is when you tell someone else you're sorry. Oftentimes, this will make things better.

A good apology should start by saying you're sorry and then continue by telling them what you think you did poorly. You might say, "I'm sorry I didn't ask you to go to the movies with us." This is a great start to an authentic apology, but it's a good idea to also recognize how you made them feel and validate the hurt you caused them. By doing this, you're also giving them a chance to feel comfortable around you again because they know that you understand the pain you caused.

You could modify your earlier statement to this: "I'm sorry I didn't ask you to go to the movies with us. I'm sure you felt left out and lonely. I don't want you to feel that way." This apology admits that you did something you shouldn't have, and it also acknowledges the other person's feelings.

Lastly, it's important to say that it won't happen again. This reassures the person you hurt that you'll be more mindful in the future.

Practice meeting each requirement of a good apology to make sure you're creating safe spaces for the people in your life.

[23]
ADAPTING TO CHANGED PLANS

Have you ever been at school and suddenly the teacher gives you a pop quiz? Can you remember how you felt and what you did?

You may have shrugged your shoulders and thought to yourself that you can handle it, adapting quickly to the stress of the unknown. Maybe you felt anxiety in your chest, or your hands started sweating. Everyone handles stress differently, especially the stress of last-minute changes. But the good news is you can learn to be comfortable with changes in the plans you made or the expectations you had for how your day was going to unfold.

The first step is to tell yourself you can handle it. You can say this to yourself or softly out loud (unless the adult in the situation has a rule for no talking, such as during a quiz). Telling yourself you're going to be okay is another option too.

Second, look for something interesting or new about the change in plans. This could even be thinking about how glad you'll be once the new plan is over. If the changed plan bothers you, you can find a safe adult and tell them. They may not be able to change the plan back to what it was, but expressing your feelings can communicate that you need more support.

Celebrate the possibilities of change whenever you can. It might feel scary and overwhelming, but it won't last forever. If you try, you can usually find something good in the new plans laid out before you.

[24]
HANDLING
BULLIES

Bullying is often verbal and emotional, but it can also be physical too. When you feel bullied by the words, actions, and behaviors of other people, it's normal to feel the urge to cry and run away. Bullies will often watch you and then figure out what they can do or say that will be most hurtful to you, so it makes sense that your feelings will be hurt.

The first thing to do is calmly get away from them as soon as you can. Don't yell or retaliate. This will be hard to do because you'll want to hurt them the way they are hurting you, but your safety is more important than getting back at them.

Once you're away from them and in a safe space, find an adult you trust who's in the building or on the property. Tell them what happened and how you felt. It's okay to cry or feel afraid. This is normal for everyone in these types of situations. Once the adult is handling the situation, do your best to avoid the bully. Keep in mind that the bully may still be in your life, so it's important to have the support of your friends and adults so that you can live your life to the fullest while also being safe.

It's important to know that even if you never see the bully again, their unkind words and behaviors may trouble you for days, weeks, or even years afterward. Try to be honest about how the bullying affected you, and talk to trusted adults about your feelings. If you see someone being bullied, go get help right away. Be sure to show kindness and friendship to the bullied person. They will be dealing with a lot of emotions and can use support, just as you would if you were in their shoes.

IMPROVING AND MAINTAINING YOUR HEALTH

[25]
STAYING ACTIVE
AND EXERCISING MORE

You may not think exercise matters at your age, but no matter how young you are, moving your body is important for your health. I can be through sports, running, playing, swimming, or dancing.

Exercise doesn't have to be done in the ways that adults in you life do it. You can find activities that make you happy and feel fun If you want to try a new sport like soccer, ballet, or basketball, tall to your parents or guardians to see if this is possible. Don't be upset if they say no. They know the budget and schedule bette than you do, so you have to trust that if they could say yes, they would.

You can always talk about alternative things you can do in you home or in your backyard that don't cost money or don't require driving. For example, you'll most likely be able to do open-ended activities like freestyle dancing. This is where you put on music you like and dance in ways that feel fun. There are videos or YouTube that show dance moves if you need inspiration. If you're allowed to play outside, you can always run, skip, jump, and race around the yard. You can even kick a soccer ball by yoursel without needing to buy a net. Use your imagination and pick a spot to be the pretend goal. Practice kicking the ball there.

You don't need to have a ton of equipment to start moving and have a great time. Be sure to move around and play every day Drink water to stay hydrated and take breaks if you feel tired.

[26]
LIMITING
SCREEN TIME

Have you ever been upset because your parents or caregivers took your phone, tablet, or TV privileges away? They probably told you that you didn't need any more "screen time" that day. Screen time is when you're sitting still with a phone, tablet, or TV turned on, and the only thing you're doing is watching. Usually, you're not even aware of what's going on around you because you're so interested in your show or movie.

Some screen time is okay, and there are so many fun things to do and watch on devices. But it can be harmful to your health if all your free time is spent alone on your devices. It's a good idea to learn how to limit screen time yourself so that you can find other activities that are fun and interesting.

If you feel yourself flipping between apps or scrolling mindlessly through YouTube or other social media platforms, chances are it's time for a break. Get up and move around, or find a sibling or parent to talk to so that you don't feel so isolated from other people.

One concern with too much time on a device is that it blocks out the human interactions happening around you. This can make you feel lonely and isolated from other people. By balancing the virtual world on devices with the real world, you'll have more balanced free time than if you were just watching a tablet or playing a game with virtual friends.

[27]
MAKING NEW FRIENDS

Some people spend most of their lives with one group of friends, while others experience life changes that result in moving away from old friends. While it is important to keep in touch with those old friends, you should also work on building new friendships too so that you have a support network locally.

Building new friendships can be difficult, particularly as we get older. We no longer bond with each other over similar interests or sharing classes in school. Finding common ground with each other can be difficult, and navigating other changes in our lives make interactions with others even more complex.

In our teenage years, making new friends becomes difficult because hormones in our bodies can make us moody, shy, or awkward. For example, you may start to feel attracted to someone at your high school, but because those feelings are new, you can feel awkward and shy. Since you don't feel like yourself, you aren't confident enough to step forward and make new friends.

As adults, making new friends is even more difficult because we lack time to socialize, and we have other obligations to consider. For example, you may have a spouse and child or a demanding job where you do not have time to go out and meet new people and make new friends.

Even though these situations can feel uncomfortable, it is always best to remind yourself that you have nothing to lose and give them a shot anyway. If you don't make an effort to build a friendship, you may just be missing out on the best friend you ever had!

[28]
MAINTAINING
HEALTHY FRIENDSHIPS

In order to have friends, you'll often need to learn how to be a good friend first. Can you tell yourself three good qualities that you're proud of having? Examples of positive qualities are patience, kindness, thoughtfulness, humor, generosity, and sensitivity. If you can't think of three qualities, ask your friends, guardians, or parents to help.

Once you have three (or more) qualities identified, focus on turning them into really strong skills. Then take those skills and use them in social situations where you're meeting new people. For example, you can show people how kind you are through your words and actions. Or you can show them how funny you are by the way you make other people smile or laugh. Knowing your good qualities will give you the confidence you need to build friendships.

For the friends you already have, the same principle applies. Are you still being generous to your friends? Are you still being sensitive to their feelings? If not, make an effort to do so.

It's easy to get to know your friends so well that you forget to be considerate of them. Part of maintaining healthy friendships is checking in with them. Ask them how they're doing. Remember to follow up if they tell you they have a big test or that their sibling is going away for a weekend. Following up to see how the test went or asking how much fun their sibling had is a great way to show you're a good listener and that you care about their life.

In addition to being considerate and a good listener, be sure to communicate with your friends if they've hurt you. Many friendships are lost due to resentment, which is when you're secretly mad or hurt but feel you can't tell the other person. Instead, you let this tension in your heart build up until the hurt becomes anger that causes you to pull away from the other person. Avoid resentment by communicating with your friend, as these relationships are an invaluable part of your life and should be cherished.

[29]
SETTING
BOUNDARIES

The word *boundary* in the context of relationships with others means a stopping point people shouldn't go past. For example, a boundary may be that you are absolutely not allowed to go into your parents' bedroom without politely knocking first. Another boundary may be that you can never say a bad word, especially in front of your grandparents.

Boundaries are put into place to let others know your limits. It's like saying, "This is a rule I have for myself that must not be broken." Most of the time, you don't set firm boundaries, but there are some areas in your life that need them. You can visualize boundaries as a circle that you draw around yourself where all the things outside the circle are okay with you, but things inside the circle are off-limits.

Maybe you don't want people to call you by a certain nickname, or maybe you don't want anyone to read your journal or diary. It could be that even though you're not allowed to lock your bedroom door, you insist on being able to lock the bathroom door. Once you've identified the boundaries you need in order to feel safe and comfortable, respectfully communicate this to others and ask for their support.

You should set boundaries when something being said or done makes you feel unsafe or bad about yourself. You deserve to feel confident and loved, and working with your friends, guardians, or teachers to create a safe space through agreed-upon boundaries is one way to accomplish this.

Boundaries are serious and need to be thought through. Your loved ones may not agree with every single boundary, and you may not agree with every one of theirs. But talking about it as a team will help alleviate some of the stress that can come with managing boundaries together.

[30]
CREATING A
HEALTHY DIET

Most foods you eat will have some healthy components. Fo
example, cereal has essential carbohydrates and minerals, while a
smoothie has important fruit and vitamins. Even a cheeseburge
has protein and dairy, both of which are important for most diets

Food can start to become unhealthy when you eat too much
causing a stomachache and weight gain due to extra calories being
stored as fat. Another issue can be not eating a variety of foods. I
someone asked you to list out your favorite foods, you could
probably do that instantly without thinking too much about it. Ir
fact, you could probably list out at least twenty things you like to
eat.

But if someone asks what you usually eat after school, you may
only eat one or two of the same snacks even though you like other
foods too. This is because humans like convenience and comfort. I
every day after school you eat applesauce, that means that the only
nutrition you receive during that time every day comes from tha
one snack. But what if one day you ate that, the next you ate a
granola bar, the next you ate peanut butter crackers, and the nex
you ate yogurt? Each snack has different things that your body
needs to be healthy. The same is true for breakfast, lunch, and
dinner. Try to eat a variety of foods so that your muscles, bones
brain, heart, and every part of your body receives the best possible
nutrition.

[31]
MAINTAINING PERSONAL HYGIENE

Personal hygiene is part of how you take care of your body. This can include taking a shower, brushing your teeth, cleaning your ears, and trimming your nails. Why do these things matter? For one thing, germs, dirt, dust, dander, and pollutants can land on your skin, in your hair, and even in your ears.

These things are normal, but they do need to be washed off even if you can't see them. In fact, you may even look at your arms and think they're clean, but that is only because most bacteria and organisms are too small for us to see.

Second, your body produces sweat and oils every day that can sometimes start to smell bad. It's a good idea to wash these off so that you don't smell.

Third, if you don't keep good hygiene, all the invisible germs and dander can sometimes make you feel tired or sick. You need to wash them off to help you stay healthy.

To start, you should always keep your hands clean. Washing your hands is not just a chore to do without a reason. Every day, you touch doorknobs, school desks, pens, the classroom furniture, and so much more. It's also healthy to wash your hands after using the restroom, before meals, and before you go to bed.

You also need to keep your teeth clean every day. It's a good idea to brush your teeth in the morning and also again at night.

Finally, if you don't take a shower after school or every day, it's a good idea to wash your feet, especially if you've been wearing sandals.

[32]
IMPROVING YOUR SELF-ESTEEM

Self-esteem is the way that we see ourselves. Each of us deserves to feel good about who we are, which includes our strengths and appearance. You can build your self-esteem in a few ways. First, it's a good idea to think nice thoughts about yourself. If you constantly have negative thoughts about yourself running through your mind, you can be on the path toward low self-esteem, shame, and deep sadness. These feelings aren't healthy and will prevent you from living a full and happy life. Instead, make sure you say nice things about yourself every day and think positive thoughts. These thoughts can either positively or negatively impact your mood. If you find yourself thinking thoughts that are so mean you would never say them to anyone else, then it's definitely time to pause and learn to be kinder.

Take a minute to stand in front of a mirror and speak kindly to yourself. Compliment yourself on what a great human you are and how much happiness you bring into other people's lives. Compliment your body and show yourself kindness no matter what anyone else may have said about you. Be sure to remind yourself how valuable you are. This world would not be the same without you, and you're needed in every area of your life.

Here are some examples of positive thoughts:

- "I am a kind person."
- "I may not have aced this test, but I will work hard and do better next time!"
- "I forgot to feed my goldfish today. It's okay to make mistakes sometimes."
- "I love my body and how it looks."
- "I am a great friend."

[33]
ASKING DOCTORS QUESTIONS

Going to the doctor can feel overwhelming, even if you're just going for a routine checkup like a yearly physical examination. Let's talk about what to expect and the types of questions you can ask during your appointment so that you can better understand what the doctor is doing during the exam.

First, the receptionist will check you in and take you into a room away from the waiting area. Then the nurse will probably weigh you and measure your height. They may also look into your ears and shine a light into your eyes to ensure both look healthy. The nurse will then check your blood pressure, gently squeezing the band around your arm with a pump to make sure all your blood is circulating the way it's supposed to. They may even take a tiny hammer and tap your knees to make sure your leg responds with a reflex motion.

Once the doctor comes in, they will read the results of the tests the nurse did on you and then ask you or your guardians some questions about your habits and any health concerns. This is to make sure you're getting the right nutrients and an adequate amount of sleep.

If you take medication, the doctor will ask you how you're feeling. It's important, to be honest, and ask questions if you have any. If the doctor is going to check something and you want to know what that means, it's okay to ask. If the doctor uses a term you haven't heard before, it's okay to ask them to explain. You should feel comfortable and safe when visiting the doctor.

[34]
GETTING ENOUGH SLEEP

On average, children can benefit from getting around 10 hours of sleep at night. This might sound like a lot, but experts agree that with so many physical and social changes happening to your body, getting enough sleep is important.

While you're asleep, your brain is doing some cool things, such as storing memories and processing thoughts. Many people think this is why humans have dreams. Your body is also hard at work at night while you're asleep. Your blood is cleaning out your body's organs, such as your heart and liver. Your muscles are recuperating and regaining their strength for the next day.

We may know that sleep is important, but how can we ensure we receive enough? First, going to bed at the same time each night is helpful. This gets your brain and body in the habit of knowing when it's time to start shutting down and conserving energy.

Have you ever noticed that you feel sleepy when it gets dark out? This is because the absence of light tells your brain it's time to sleep. In your bedroom, turning off the lights and avoiding your tablet, phone, and TV will all help your brain go to sleep.

Many kids have lots of thoughts they want to share right at bedtime. This is normal. Your mind wants to get everything out so that you can start the next day with lots of space to fill it with new thoughts. Choosing the two biggest thoughts to share is a way to get to sleep on time and clear out your mind. Sometimes, you may even feel a burst of energy and want to giggle or run around right before crashing into bed and falling asleep.

[35]
PROTECTING YOURSELF
FROM ALLERGIES

It can be hard when something hurts, and you can't quite explain it, even as adults are asking you to tell them how you feel. This is especially true when an allergy comes out of nowhere and starts to cause your skin, head, or stomach to hurt.

It's normal to feel frustrated when you can't explain what's going on or you can't remember what you ate to upset your stomach. Take a deep breath and tell yourself it's going to be okay. You'll figure it out.

An allergy occurs when your body responds negatively to something in your environment. This can be pollen in the air, which is referred to as seasonal allergies, or it could be another type of allergen like food. Allergies can cause sneezing, headaches, or other severe reactions.

Seasonal allergies that you feel each spring or fall can usually be handled with an allergy pill. You may feel uncomfortable for a while, but that will usually go away with medicine. On the other hand, food allergies tend to be more serious. They may last for your whole life, and the best way to handle them is to be very careful about what you eat.

If you're feeling unwell after eating or drinking something, be sure to talk to your parents or caregivers right away. Tell them how you feel and let them know the sick feeling happened right after lunch or eating a snack. This can help the adults in your life determine if they need to take you to the doctor or if they want to wait and see if it happens again. It may not be the food itself. You may be allergic to the food coloring or a small ingredient. All of this is very common, and you can work with your guardians to figure it out and stay safe.

[36]
REACTING WHEN
SOMETHING IS UNSAFE

Even though you aren't yet an adult, your opinions and ideas are important. This is especially true if you notice that something isn't safe. This can be at home, at school, in the car, or anywhere. If you see something, say something.

Let's say that your brother has diabetes and needs to use a machine to read his blood sugar. If you haven't seen the device as your family is laying out items to take to the zoo, ask whether anyone remembered to bring it along. Even if it turns out there's a second one they've already packed, you're still being aware of safety by thinking about which tools your brother needs to be healthy.

Safety also involves being aware of your surroundings. If you're at the playground and your parent leaves their bag behind to help your sister, you could go sit by it to make sure no one takes it.

Sometimes, people say hurtful things about others. This can make you upset, and it's okay to let the adults in your life know what was said and why you felt unsafe. Someone may not have physically done something unsafe, but if they made you feel unsafe because of how they talk about others, then it's still important to bring that up.

A great way to promote safety at home is to ask your caregivers or parents what they want you to do if there's a fire, a stranger at the door, a dog running loose in your yard, or someone online trying to send you messages. Being safe is something your whole household can talk about.

[37]
BEING PREPARED ON THE GO

You may not carry a first aid kit around with you everywhere you go, but you can learn where the first aid kits are in the places you usually visit. Take a moment and talk to your guardians about where the first aid kit is, what's inside it, and how to use those supplies. There is usually a first aid kit in your home, but it's a good idea to also have one in the car. Hopefully, you go through your whole life and never need to use a first aid kit, but knowing how to use one can make a big difference if you need it. At school, make sure you know how to get to the nurse's office and ask your teacher where the first aid kit is in the classroom. If there isn't one, ask where things like Band-Aids might be.

Common things you'll find in a first aid kit may include Band-Aids, alcohol wipes to clean a scrape or small cut, gauze to stop bleeding, and a larger bandage to wrap around an arm or leg.

You can also carry your own supplies. For example, if you know that your period could happen unexpectedly, you might want to keep menstrual supplies in your backpack or locker.

EXPLORING RECREATIONAL ACTIVITIES

[38]
TRYING NEW
ACTIVITIES

Trying new things is usually a fun experience, even if the things you're trying are labeled as "healthy" or look like something you wouldn't normally enjoy. Healthy things can include sports, games, friends, or hobbies.

For example, it's normal to look at a new food and think it might not taste good. But imagine if you looked at a chocolate chip cookie for the first time and you thought that the chocolate pieces looked like big lumps of dirt. You would never have tried the cookie, and it would be a shame to miss out on something good just because it may not look appealing at first.

The next time you see a food that doesn't look very good but it's something your family or health class teacher says is healthy, at least take a bite and try to keep an open mind. Things like blueberries or cantaloupe may look strange, but you never know how much you might end up liking them after giving them a try.

The same is true for sports and games. They may look hard, or you may see the other kids playing who are really tired or sweaty. It's easy to say to yourself that you don't like sports even before trying a few to see if there's one you like. Trying a sport out for half an hour might be the perfect way to start a lifelong love of an activity or hobby.

Sometimes, it isn't distaste for something that holds you back. It can also be fear. You might be afraid to try something new because

ou didn't like the last healthy thing you tried. You may be afraid
hat playing a sport will hurt you, or you'll fall, and everyone will
augh. These fears are usually so much worse in your mind than
hey are in real life. You'll be surprised at how often they don't
ven come true!

[39]
JOINING A
SPORTS TEAM

There are many group activities that are fun and healthy for you
o do. These can include hobbies like playing with Legos or more
raditional sports such as bowling, swimming, or basketball. All of
hese can be done with other people, either on a team or in a group
etting where you each participate individually in the same
ctivity. Let's talk about how to join a group activity or a sports
eam.

First, tell your parents or guardians you want to join and why. If
ou've tried it and you had a great time, they will probably say yes
nd let you do it again. If you've never tried it, then they may want
ou to do a short trial in the hobby or sport first to make sure you
ike it before committing to being on a team.

Next, learn everything you can about the hobby or sport. Practice
t at home and set goals for how to improve even before you join
he group or team.

After that, you'll want to know the groups or teams available to
oin through school or the community. You'll most likely need to

buy some basic equipment and learn what times and how often practice will be. You'll also need to know if there are any competitions involved and whether they require travel. You and your parents or caregivers can decide if the requirements fit into your family's schedule.

Once you join the team or group, it's important to be nice to the other kids on your team. It's okay if you're the new kid or you don't have a lot of experience yet. Keep a good attitude and try your hardest during practice. Be sure to listen to your coaches, and let your guardians know if anyone on the team isn't being nice to you.

Hopefully, you'll still love the hobby or sport at the end of the season, but if not, that's okay too. You tried your best and saw it through to the end.

[40]
STICKING TO
A HOBBY

Many kids will start a hobby but then lose interest or stop finding it fun after a while. This can be frustrating not only for you but also for the adults in your life who bought you the tools and gear you needed. Luckily, there are ways you can stay interested in a hobby long after the initial thrill or excitement is over.

First, try to figure out why you're losing interest. Imagine that you really wanted to learn how to paint. Your parents told you it was a hard skill to learn, but you were convinced that you wanted to do it. In your mind, you saw yourself painting all the intricate and cool paintings in the book they bought you. But in real life, you learned very quickly that it would take you years to be that good.

Once you realized it would not take a long time, you became discouraged. You may still like to paint, but you don't want to do it anymore because you aren't where you want to be. This can be hard to tell your parents, let alone figure out yourself. But if you sit with your feelings and ask yourself why you don't want to keep trying, you may eventually get to this answer.

Once you figure out why you lost motivation, find a smaller goal or some fun things about the hobby that still excite you and make you want to try again. Usually, just setting smaller goals is enough to help you keep going.

Finding a friend who is on the same level as you and who can talk about the hobby with you is also a good way to keep yourself happy. Hobbies are important for kids and adults alike, so starting one when you're young can keep you occupied for years.

[41]
READING
BOOKS

Reading is a skill that you can learn and then get better at doing. While some people enjoy reading the books they're assigned in school, it's even better to read books you choose yourself.

Choose books that are about topics you enjoy. If you love pirate stories, then you'll read better by picking up a pirate adventure book. If you like a certain TV series, find out if they have the book version written for your age group.

As you read, it's possible you'll still find words you can't figure out right away. If you're allowed, take a pencil and underline the words that you can't say or pronounce well. Don't worry about them until the end of the story when you can, ask an adult what the word means or look it up online. Sometimes, you can still follow the story without knowing every word right away. Waiting until the end to receive help with a few words is more fun than having to stop and wait for help as you're reading.

[42]
RIDE A BIKE
OR SKATE

Riding a bicycle means you get to go faster than you could if you were running, which is a lot of fun. The first thing you need when riding a bike is protective gear such as a helmet, knee pads, and elbow pads. These things will keep your head, knees, and elbows protected in case of an accident.

If you never learned to ride a bicycle, you might be able to find training wheels to keep your bike upright and prevent you from falling to the side. With training wheels, you can focus on learning how to steer and stop the bike using the brakes. If training wheels aren't available for your size bicycle, ride slowly and carefully as you're starting out to help keep your balance.

Most bicycles have foot brakes, but your bike may have hand brakes too. Practice using brakes at a low speed first. Remember to look both ways before turning, leaving your driveway, going near a street, or changing directions.

When learning how to skate, similar rules apply. Wear your helmet, knee pads, and elbow pads for safety. Learn how to stand upright on your skates first by holding onto something that won't move. Move your legs forward and backward and see how the skates respond. It's okay to fall down a few times until you learn.

Make sure you never learn to skate on a busy road or near cars. Skating isn't easy to learn, and you need to do so in a safe area away from traffic. If you have an indoor roller-skating rink nearby, this is often a great place to learn because you can use the training walls and/or walkers to help you stay upright. Have fun, but practice in appropriate locations.

[43]
FISHING OR HUNTING

Fishing and hunting are activities to do with a trusted adult. It's not a good idea to try to fish or hunt without adult supervision. In fact, it's illegal in many states for a minor under the age of 16 to hold a weapon, even when hunting with an adult. Be sure your parents or guardians know the laws in your state and wait until you're old enough.

Be sure to wear gear that has reflectors on it and follow all instructions carefully. If the adult with you tells you it's time to be quiet, trust that they have a good reason for it. If they tell you not to go into a certain area, trust that it's for your own safety. Fishing and hunting are dangerous, and following the rules will help keep everyone safer.

[44]
USING A
COMPASS

Compasses have a needle that is oriented in a direction that points towards the magnetic North of the Earth. A compass has a revolving dial that you may turn to determine your direction and a base with degrees inscribed.

The needle of the compass points to the magnetic North, which is somewhat different from the true North or the North Pole. Magnetic North is indicated by the direction that the needle points.

To use a compass to find a direction, hold it flat in your palm so that it is parallel to the ground. Make the necessary adjustments to get the needle to align with the "N" on the dial. The direction arrow at the bottom of the compass currently points in a northerly direction. Take advantage of this information to get your bearings on the map.

To ensure that the map accurately depicts the surrounding environment, set the compass on top of the map in such a way that he base's outer edge points in the desired direction. Together, rotate the map and the compass until the needle on the compass points toward the North.

[45]
DRAW OR
PAINT

Have you ever seen a pretty flower or watched a sunset and thought how great it would be to paint it so that you can capture the moment and hang it on your bedroom wall? Most people have thought about drawing or painting at some point in their lives.

Learning to draw is a great first step toward starting to paint. Drawing can give you an outline of what you want to fill in with paints. For example, if you want to paint a flower, you can start by tracing the outline of a real flower. Then you can try again without the flower outline and draw it from memory. The more you draw without tracing something, the better you can become.

There are two things to think about when drawing or painting. The first is the dimension of the object. This just means how you make it look three-dimensional on paper, as if there's a real flower sitting there. You can learn to give it dimension by adding shadows, which is not hard to do.

To start with, all the parts that are near the bottom can have a shadow. A shadow is just shading along the outline at the bottom, and it's usually made with darker grays or blues to give it weight. The second thing to think about is how big the flower is compared to the table it's sitting on. Getting the proportions of each object in your drawing correct can make it look more real.

Another tip is to study the flower you're using as a model. It may look like it's just a white or blue flower to you, but if you look closer, you'll see shades of color from yellow to orange. Adding these accents will help your drawing or painting look very detailed and realistic.

[46]
PLAYING AND
APPRECIATING MUSIC

Music can put us in a happy, playful, thoughtful, or relaxed mood. Chances are you like many types of music and don't even realize it. You may start out listening to pop or dance music because that's what you hear in your favorite TV shows, but there are many other types of music.

Some other examples include rock, classical, jazz, R&B, and country. Each one has a different style and makes you feel a different way. The next time you're listening to music, try asking if anyone can suggest new genres. You may be surprised how much you enjoy every style of music.

If you're becoming interested in music, you may want to learn to play an instrument. A musical instrument is usually just one part of the sound that you hear when listening to the radio. You may hear three guitars, drums, and a piano all at once in a song. If you see a guitarist on stage in a TV show and want to give it a try, you can usually do this by taking a lesson in a music store. However, you may discover that you don't like guitar very much after all and then try the piano.

Eventually, you'll probably find an instrument you like and that you think you'll enjoy practicing again and again. The people you listen to on the radio have practiced for years to be as good as they are. You can, too, with enough practice and determination.

PREPARING FOR THE FUTURE

[47]
MANAGING
YOUR MONEY

As you grow up and learn about money, how to make money, and how to invest or save it, you should ask the adults in your life for advice. You can consult your older siblings, guardians, cousins, or grandparents.

You'll find that each person has a different idea of how money should be used. Some people want to save most of it and put it into an investment so that it makes more money back for them. Other people want to feel like they're living life to the very best, so they spend more money than they save. You can start figuring out your ideas about money now. It takes time and effort to make money, so be careful how quickly you decide what to do with it.

A good rule of thumb is to first use your money on the things that are essential. Every family situation is different, but if you receive money as an allowance or as a birthday gift, chances are you have some freedom on where it gets spent. If it's up to you to buy the thing you need to start a new sport or hobby, then that could be an example of an essential item.

Maybe all your essential things are already purchased by your guardians. In this case, try to save over half your money and allow yourself to buy something nonessential that you really want. You can also save up to buy something bigger that you want but will need a few more months or weeks to have enough money to buy.

Many adults might have a hard time saying no to the things they want. Starting young and telling yourself no will teach you how to spend money responsibly in adulthood.

[48]
DISAGREEING
POLITELY

When you think someone is wrong or lying, it can be easy to raise your voice at them or become angry. When someone does something to hurt you, it's tempting to cry or run away and tell an adult without trying to figure out what actually happened from the other person's perspective.

When disagreements happen, it's okay to try and understand what the other person is thinking or why they're doing something in a way that you think is incorrect. You can do this politely and without accusations if you ask them why without making them feel like they're wrong. You'll see that most of the time, they have good intentions or just made a mistake. You might also see that your teammate wasn't mad at you when they spoke to you unkindly. They were actually mad at themselves for missing a goal.

Speaking politely lets you get to the bottom of the issue a little quicker than yelling or running away. If you don't feel safe in a disagreement, then staying around the unsafe person to understand their behaviors isn't a good idea. In this instance, you would want to find a safe and trusted adult to help figure out the issue.

[49]
ACCEPTING
CRITICISM

If you were asked about your opinion on a movie you watched recently, you might talk about things you liked and didn't like about it. You'd be able to talk about the aspects of the story that were boring and discuss your favorite parts.

This happens in other parts of life too. People have opinions on things you do, say, wear, and even how you look. When someone gives their opinion, that can be considered criticism. Criticism is when someone points out that you did something wrong or not up to a certain standard.

As you can imagine, criticism is a normal part of life. It may be hard to take criticism when, deep inside, you're upset at the words someone else is saying. Let's talk about how to accept criticism.

First, know that not everything people think about you is accurate. Just because someone doesn't like something you're doing or wearing doesn't mean you're a bad person or that they have the right to criticize you. You should listen to parents and teachers if they tell you you're breaking a rule, but don't take everyone's opinion so seriously that it lowers your self-esteem.

Second, it's usually a good idea to listen politely, even if you disagree. Finally, talk to someone you trust about the criticism and make sure you only take away the valid feedback.

[50]
ASKING FOR
HELP

If you don't know how to do something or you need help learning a new skill, it's okay to ask a trusted person for help. Receiving help can speed up the learning process, as listening to someone answer your questions can teach you how to do something new. Receiving help can also empower you to then turn around and assist others because you know how important it can be.

Let's say that you're in a new school and you can't remember where the cafeteria is, or you can't find your next class. You might feel shy and not want to ask a stranger for help, but there's an easy way to find the right words to say.

First, if you're interrupting someone, you can say, "I'm sorry to interrupt." Then you can let them know who you are and what the problem is. For example, you can say, "My name is Max. I'm new here, and I can't find the cafeteria." Then ask for what you need. "Can you point me in the right direction?" You can use this formula for many things you may need help with.

[51]
WRITING A
LETTER

Sometimes, you may need to sit down, take out a pen and a piece of paper, and write a letter. You could write a letter to your grandparents, invite someone to your birthday party, or keep in touch with a friend who has moved far away. While the words in your letter will differ each time, the structure will usually be the same.

First, start your letter with a greeting. This can be *Dear John* or *Hi Tamara* or anything that feels comfortable to you. Then you need to start a new line and let them know why you're writing the letter. You can say that you're thinking of them or inviting them to a party.

Continue with the topic of your letter for the next several sentences. If it's a letter to a friend who has moved, you can fill them in on all the fun things that have been happening. If it's an invitation, you can give them details such as where and when the event will be.

At the very end, once you're finished telling them each detail, you can write a closing wishing them well and then sign your name at the bottom.

[52]
SENDING A
FORMAL E-MAIL

An email is similar in structure to a letter. You want to have a greeting, state the purpose of the email, elaborate on the purpose, and then sign your email at the end.

However, there are a few rules to keep in mind with formal emails. First, make sure you type in the correct email address of the person in the recipient bar at the top of your email. Second, be aware that emails last forever, so anything you type should be truthful and kind. Finally, keep in mind that people don't always receive their emails if they're mismarked as spam. The spam folder collects email messages from people who aren't in the receiver's contact list or who have never emailed them before. People can click on their spam folder and see all the emails that were automatically put there, so if you haven't heard back in a while, this could be the reason why.

When you're emailing your friends, you may use very casual and friendly words or poor punctuation, and that's okay. But when you're sending a formal email, it's always a good idea to use correct punctuation and structure the email as discussed earlier.

[53]
MAILING A
PACKAGE

It can be a lot of fun to receive a package in the mail, and it's just as fun to send a package to someone else. There are a few different ways to send a package. You can send it express, meaning that it will get to the other person very quickly. You can also send it to them standard, where it will get to them in about a week.

You can also choose the type of box the package goes in. Some stores where people ship packages have brightly colored boxes in different sizes that you can choose from, while others have different sizes but one color.

You want to put the items you're sending in a box that doesn't have a lot of empty space once it's closed and taped. Make sure the items you are shipping are legal and okay to ship, and ensure anything valuable has bubble wrap around it.

You need to write or print the mailing address of the person you're sending the package to, usually at their home address. Sometimes, this can be an apartment or condo. The mailing address may look a little different from yours. Make sure to put your own address on the box in the top left-hand corner in case the package gets sent back to you. It's usually nice to include a card or note inside the package to let the person know why you're sending it.

[54]
GIVING PROPER
CHANGE

Cash isn't as popular as credit cards, but many people still use cash for ordinary transactions. If you pay with cash, you'll probably receive coins or bills back in return as change. People receive change back when the paper bills they give to the cashier are worth more than the cost of the items they're buying.

For example, if groceries cost $18.10 and you give the cashier a $20 bill, then the cashier will give you back $1.90.

It's important to know how to calculate how much change you should receive to make sure the change is accurate. There may be instances where you are selling cookies for your school or group and need to make change for a customer. Look at the amount of money they gave you and then subtract the actual cost of the item. The difference is what you give back. You start with the largest bill first, and then you add in the coins at the end.

[55]
SAYING NO
TO SOMETHING
DANGEROUS

Let's talk about what the word *dangerous* means. Something i
dangerous when it can harm someone, like jumping off a tal
bridge into a creek below. The person could land on a rock in the
water and injure themselves. Touching a hot stovetop is dangerou:
because you can get burned, and it would hurt quite badly
Bullying is dangerous because it can hurt someone for many year:
after the mean words are said.

These are only a few examples of things that are dangerous, and
you can probably think of many more right now. It might be easy
to say no to putting your hand on a hot stovetop, but it may not be
as easy to avoid cheating on a test, joining in on teasing the new
kid in class, or playing a prank on someone when all your friend:
want to do it.

The first thing to ask yourself is, "Would I want this done to me?"
Even if everyone else is doing it and they make it sound fun, if it':
something you wouldn't want done to you, then that's ar
immediate no. The second thing to ask is, "Would I do this if adult:
were standing right there watching me?" If the answer is no, ther
don't do it. The third thing to consider is, "Will this hurt someone
either physically or emotionally?" If the answer is yes, then don'
do it. Even if you aren't sure, it's still best to say no.

[56]
COPING WITH
FAILURE

Failure is when you don't meet expectations or achieve your goals. Sometimes, expectations are making straight A's all school year, getting off the bench on the sports team, or moving to a more advanced level in your violin classes by the end of the school year.

If you set a goal or expectation for yourself to get straight A's all year, you know you'll need to study and put effort into meeting that goal. If you get all A's except for one class, you might consider this a failure and feel bad about yourself, but you still achieved most of your goals.

If you failed to reach an expectation, take a look at the work you put into reaching that goal. Surely, you'll find something that you can be proud of. It's okay to start planning to reach your goal in the next year and start working toward it.

Even if you feel disappointed, sad, or upset, keep in mind that most people don't reach every expectation set for them, and it's okay to be imperfect. Make sure you try your best and then accept the results.

[57]
REMAINING RESILIENT WHEN THINGS DON'T GO YOUR WAY

Being resilient means that even if you stumble in life, you can recover your self-esteem, courage, and determination. People who are resilient understand that they won't win every time and know that it's important to get back up and press onward. If something doesn't go your way, it's normal to feel sad or disappointed, but don't sit on those feelings for too long or let them turn into shame.

It's normal to mess up occasionally or not get what you want, but that's not a reflection of who you are and what you have to offer the world. It's a good idea to find someone to talk to when you mess up so that you can express how you feel. Hopefully, they can encourage you to try again or attempt something new.

When something doesn't go your way at school, at home, or while playing sports, the temptation to throw a fit or pout may be tempting. This will not help you, nor will it help anyone else. Instead, try to calm down and think positive thoughts. If you identified what you did that wasn't quite right, then decide not to do it again. If the outcome had nothing to do with your effort, then accept it and move on.

[58]
STANDING UP
FOR OTHERS

When was the last time someone defended you, supported you, or stood up for you? Can you remember what they said or did that made you feel so much better? Chances are you can remember a lot of details about that moment. When we're feeling down or left out, the kindness of others sticks with us and can encourage us long after the moment has passed.

We can do this for other people too. If someone at school is being teased about the clothes they're wearing or their accent, you can support them. You can tell them you like their accent, or you think their shoes are cool. They might still turn away when you do this, but if you follow up with more words of kindness the next time you see them, their attitude may soften, and they may believe your words.

The thing to remember about being kind is that it's not something we can do just once and expect the impact to last a lifetime. We need to be kind each day.

If you're in a group of friends and they are teasing someone, you can speak your opinion right there on the spot and let them know you disagree and then explain your thoughts. This will challenge the way they're speaking and make the person being teased feel supported.

[59]
BEING
RESPONSIBLE

Being responsible means, you'll take care of your responsibilities every day, not just once in a while or when you feel like it. Being consistent with your responsibilities will help make you a responsible person. Take a moment to write down the things that you oversee at home and at school. Then ask yourself how often you do those things and if there are some you can do better.

Next, ask yourself which of these tasks or chores you enjoy doing more than others and which ones you don't like at all. If you focus on responsibilities you dislike, you might be able to find ways to make them more fun. If you do the least fun chores or tasks first, you can have the freedom to do things you enjoy later.

For example, if you enjoy vacuuming as one of your chores, but you really don't like putting laundry away, try tackling the laundry and then rewarding yourself by doing something you like afterward. This can be an activity like texting a friend or listening to your favorite song.

[60]
RAISING AND
CARING FOR A
PET

Pets can be so much fun to play with, but they also need exercise, food, water, and attention. Have you ever had a pet before? If so, then you may remember all the work your parents or guardians put into making sure your pet had a good life in your home. If not, then think about all the things you need in your life in order to be happy, and then imagine all the things a pet would need in theirs.

Pets such as dogs and cats have their own preferences, needs, likes, and dislikes. A pet may prefer a special toy over all others, or they may like one member of the household more than the rest.

When your family gets a pet, pay close attention to your responsibilities in caring for your new companion. If it's your job to provide it with water, then make sure you're consistent with this chore. If you need to brush the family dog each Saturday, then make sure you learn how to do this well.

Usually, a pet will need food each day and a full water bowl. Some animals need to be let outside to use the bathroom in the yard. Their poop will need to be picked up and put in the trash, and they will also need playtime or walks. It can be a lot of work, but having a pet is well worth it!

[61]
USING THE
INTERNET

You probably have a family computer, or you may have a laptop, tablet, or phone of your own. These devices use the internet to access search engines, social media, video games, and many other fun things.

Make sure to ask your guardians first before accessing an unknown page or downloading a new app. Once you're using an app or a search engine, there are still ways that you may be put in harm's way. First, never message strangers or use video apps that match you with random people unless your parents have given you permission. These types of apps and platforms are popular but they also let people into your life. They can either see your room or home on camera, or they could try to ask personal questions when messaging. Protect yourself by never doing these activities alone or without the approval of a responsible adult in your life.

If something is popular at school, but your parents say they don't want you to use it, then you need to trust them and avoid doing it for your own safety. Instead, you can enjoy the many apps that are safe to use and connect with your friends and peers that way.

Everyone wants to try the latest fun trend, but it's often safer not to engage if you aren't positive about the risk. Safety is critically important whenever you're online.

[62]
STAYING SAFE
AROUND STRANGERS

The adults you live with have experienced quite a bit more than you, so when they give rules about safety around strangers, it's because they know that, sadly, not every person is kind or caring. Sometimes, people can be dangerous and not worthy of your trust. That's why you should follow all the rules your family has put in place regarding strangers or being in public places.

It's also true that sometimes people may look like they're up to no good when in reality, they aren't causing harm. For example, someone may seem like they're following you and your family around the grocery store, but then you realize they work for a food delivery service and they happen to be buying similar items. Even in this instance where it turns out someone isn't trying to cause harm in the end, you should still follow your family's safety rules.

An important rule to stay safe around strangers is to never reveal if you're alone. If you're standing outside school waiting to be picked up and a strange adult asks you if your guardian is there yet, it's okay to immediately walk away to an adult you know and trust. You don't have to say you're alone.

Never leave anywhere with a stranger, regardless of what they say. Don't feel that you must answer any of their questions about who you are, where you live, or what your name is. Stay alert and be aware of who is around you and what they're doing.

[63]
USING PROPER GRAMMAR

There's a difference between using good grammar and using slang words. When you're speaking with friends, you probably use words that are considered slang. It might be fun to speak in trendy slang words with friends or your siblings, but learning to use proper grammar is a skill that takes time to perfect.

There is a time and a place to use slang words and a time and a place to use proper grammar. This is true for speaking, texting, or written communication. You may be thinking there's no point for you to speak with proper grammar at your age, but the reality is that you should have this skill set just in case you need it. Using proper grammar will help you when you're in school, speaking with adults, or getting your first job.

BEING A
POSITIVE INFLUENCE

[64]
INSPIRING
KINDNESS

Kindness is doing nice things without expecting anything in return because you want the other person to feel happy and receive something awesome in their life. Some examples of kindness are holding the door open for someone, inviting the new kid to eat lunch with your friends, and refilling the cat's water bowl when you see that your brother forgot to.

Take a moment to recall the last time someone did something kind for you and how it made you feel. Then think of one kind thing you can do today for your loved ones. Do something you know they'll like.

Kindness can be planned, like coordinating a surprise birthday party for your grandpa, or it can be spontaneous. The cool thing about kindness is that other people can tell you that you're being helpful without wanting anything, and that, in turn, can fill up their heart with kindness.

Kindness, like meanness, can spread quickly. When we spread kindness, it makes everyone's lives a little bit better every single time.

[65]
SEEING OTHER
PEOPLE'S PERSPECTIVES

Many of our disagreements come from not understanding how another person is thinking or feeling and not even listening to them when they try to explain. Listening to someone explain their opinions when you disagree with them is part of seeing something from their perspective. When you finally "get it" in terms of how they think or feel, you can more easily come to a result that you both are okay with.

For example, if your sister is mad at you for jumping up and down behind her and making funny faces while she is video-chatting with her best friend, but you think it was just a funny thing to do, you should listen to why it upset her. Maybe she was talking about something personal, and that's why she was mad at you for jumping in her call. Maybe she was embarrassed because the girl she was talking to was not her best friend but a popular girl from school.

Until you ask and try to understand other people's feelings, you'll just think they're being rude for no reason. Listening to their words will help you decide if you want to change your behavior or if it isn't fair for them to ask you to change.

[66]
ADMITTING
WHEN YOU'RE
WRONG

If you're anything like most people, you've probably been certain you were right about something only to later discover you were completely wrong. This is normal, and it just happens sometimes. Maybe you said something you thought was innocent, only to discover you greatly offended someone.

There are times in your life when you'll need to think about your words or actions and admit to someone else that you were in the wrong. Each of us must do that from time to time, and it's a healthy thing to do.

First, if someone accuses you of being in the wrong about something, take a calm breath and clear your thoughts. Your first reaction is probably to argue with them, but instead, try staying calm and make sure you're ready to listen. Next, listen to what they have to say.

Don't interrupt, and try to understand their complaints. If you agree with them because they can show you factually that you're wrong, then simply agree and move on. But if it's the case where feelings are involved, and they can't prove to you that you hurt their feelings, then try to imagine how you would feel if you were them.

Once you can show them empathy, take a minute to think through what you'll say. Admit that you can see how your words or actions were hurtful and shouldn't be repeated. Most of the time, admitting you're wrong is the first step to restoring peace between you and the other person. Usually, you'll apologize afterward and restore good feelings.

[67]
BECOMING
MORE ACCEPTING

Each of us is raised in a unique way that's very different from others. What we believe, how we're taught to act, and the ways we see adults acting and speaking at home will be different. It's understandable that you might want to rush in and tell someone that they're wrong because they have different habits, beliefs, or thoughts.

This can make others feel disrespected because you're not acknowledging their upbringing or culture. Instead, it's much wiser to listen to what they have to say and ask polite questions to understand further. Usually, you can find common areas to align on different ideas or parts of an idea.

Sometimes, different ideas come from other people having very different personalities. The same rules apply: Listen first and ask questions to better understand. When it's your turn to speak, you can express how you want things to be done and then work to compromise.

[68]
COMFORTING OTHERS

Occasionally, we may feel sad, or a depressing life event may have happened to us. Examples of this can be when a friend moves away to a different state or when a family trip is canceled or postponed.

If someone you know is hurting or sad, remember how you felt during those times. Think of all the ways your parents or close friends helped you feel better. Then offer to help someone else in those same ways. This could be through listening to them talk about their feelings or offering to spend time together to help them take their mind off things for a little while.

If it's appropriate, you might offer to give them a hug. Most often, just being with them is the most positive way you can offer comfort. It's normal for people not to want to talk about what's hurting them right away because it feels too painful, so be sure not to push them to talk.

You can start by saying you notice they aren't quite themselves or that they seem a little sad. Point out you're there for them if they want to talk. You can also walk with them to talk to their parents, a teacher, or a counselor at school to show support.

SUCCEEDING
IN SCHOOL

[69]
STUDYING
EFFECTIVELY

Until the day you graduate, you'll be faced with tests where your teachers determine how much information you're retaining. Tests or quizzes can be stressful, and studying for them can increase your feelings of anxiety. Think about the last time you sat down to study. How did you feel? If you felt bored, unmotivated, or impatient, then maybe your methods for studying just weren't the right fit for you.

Many people will sit down to study a large amount of information all at once and spend an hour or more on it, hoping they'll remember it on the day of the test. This might work for some people but not for everyone. Next time, try to study for 15 or 20 minutes every single day instead of an hour all at once. This will allow your brain to see the information daily but not in a way that will feel overwhelming.

You can also try to visualize the information in pictures. For example, if you're struggling with spelling the word *orangutan*, picture the animal in your mind with the correct letters underneath it. Another method to help you study is to have someone you trust ask you questions about the material and have you "teach" or explain it to them. By teaching others, you might learn the material better.

Finally, be kind to yourself. Choose to think positive thoughts about your ability to remember the information.

[70]
GETTING ALONG WITH TEACHERS

It can be hard to think about your teachers as ordinary people. Since they're older than you, you probably assume they can't see things from your perspective or that they can't understand you. Underneath the differences in age, background, or personality traits is a human just like you.

If you find you're not getting along with your teacher or that they seem to be singling you out for negative feedback, try to learn what they expect from their students. Look at their class rules and make sure you're following them. Ensure you're respectful in class and that you're doing your work as well as you can.

It's okay to say hello to your teachers as you walk into class or if you see them in the hallways. Even if they may not walk around smiling all the time, that doesn't mean they don't appreciate a greeting or a smile. Many teachers have a big heart for helping kids learn new things.

Be sure to open your mind in class. You can respectfully ask questions if you don't understand, and make sure to listen carefully to the answers your teacher gives you. Always try your

best, and don't take corrections to your work personally. Teacher
want what's best for you.

[71]
AVOIDING
GOSSIP

Gossip is when you talk about other people's business when it isn'
yours to tell. This is oftentimes done in a negative or hurtful way.

If you are merely giving your friends an update on a friend wh
hasn't been in school for a while, that isn't gossip. Giving a
update is using factual information, such as telling someone you
friend Laura caught a cold at school on Monday and won't be bac
until Wednesday.

Gossip is when you take it further than that and start to te
everyone how sick Laura was, who got her sick, or how she looke
as she was leaving school on Monday. Those are personal detail
that only Laura should tell.

If you find yourself in a situation where people around you ar
gossiping about others, you can silently wait for them to b
finished and then change the subject to talk about something else
If you know the people who are gossiping very well, then you ca
tell them directly that they're gossiping and you would rather tal
about something else.

It isn't always a good idea to confront people when gossip is happening. You shouldn't try to correct people you don't know well or people who are much older than you. Usually, it's enough to simply wait to speak until the gossip is finished. However, if you notice that gossip is happening a lot with the same people, it's okay to spend less time with them and find friends who speak nicely of others.

[72]
KNOWING WHEN
TO GET INVOLVED

If something dangerous or unsafe is happening around you, your first instinct might be to step in immediately and try to help. Sometimes, this is exactly the best thing to do but not always. There are many things to think about before you involve yourself in problems or danger around you.

Examples of dangerous situations could be someone pushing a student at school out of sight of the teachers, someone in the grocery store parking lot yelling at a stranger, or a big dog you don't recognize running down the street with its leash trailing behind it. Each of these situations could potentially be dangerous, and it's important to check your options before stepping in.

First, look around and see if there are any adults you trust in the area. If there are, quietly go to them and allow them to handle the situation. If there aren't, can you think of a place nearby where an adult would be? Go find the adult and tell them what's going on.

Second, assess how likely it is that you'll be hurt if you step in. One person getting hurt is awful enough, but you might get hurt, too, if you intervene. If you think you may be hurt by stepping in, then go find help.

Third, once an adult is present and handling the situation, stay out of the way so that you don't prevent the adult from doing what they need to do.

[73]
IMPROVING YOUR ATTENTION SPAN

We live during a time when there are so many electronic devices to interact with. Whether you're watching a show, playing a game, or reading an article, there are many things you can do on your devices.

It's important to keep in mind that the content we watch can be very short and can train our brains to expect an entire conversation to happen just as quickly in real life. As a result, it's common to get bored quickly when you must watch, listen, read, or interact with things that last longer than a few minutes.

Let's talk about ways you can make your attention span last longer, which is important because your brain needs both short bursts and longer ones to operate at its best.

If you're reading a book or researching information and find your mind wandering, you can set a short goal of reading one whole page and then doing something physical. This can be wiggling your toes, stretching, or jumping up and down before going right back to reading. Doing these physical activities will force your brain to rest.

Gradually, you'll be able to increase the length of time you're focusing. If you're in a conversation and find yourself bored, try asking questions about the topic to reengage yourself or allow your eyes to glance away before returning to the speaker. You can also try to focus on only one of your senses when you feel your mind wander. This can help your mind take a break before returning your full focus to the task at hand.

[74]
IMPROVING
WEAKER SUBJECTS

Most students have that one subject in school that's more challenging than others. For many, it can be math or remembering all the dates and people in history class. If you have a subject that's very hard for you, try these ways to make it feel easier.

First, tell yourself that you're smart, and you can figure it out. Second, identify which part of the class is most challenging. Is it remembering facts or formulas, or is it something else entirely? You'll have a better chance at fixing your issue if you can find the thing that's most difficult.

Third, ask for help coming up with a plan to solve the problem you just identified. Examples of plans can include changing your study habits, getting a new homework routine in place, or finding more time to work through homework.

Finally, ask your teacher or another adult for help. Try to do the steps above first so that when you do ask for help, you know exactly what you're struggling with. Oftentimes, teachers have tricks to help their students do better in class. They can explain the subject in a new or different way, or they can show you techniques to help the information stay in your mind longer.

[75]
RETAINING INFORMATION

Forgetting things you learned in school is normal. However, there are some ways you improve how much you retain from class.

First, make sure you aren't sitting in class and getting distracted by other students, the posters or signs on the walls, or the sounds in the hallways. Second, don't let your brain distract you with thoughts of the past or the future. Try to be in the present moment and keep your mind clear. Distracting thoughts could include thinking about what you want to eat for lunch, the big game you have coming up in sports, or wondering why someone in your last class said or did something. These thoughts can prevent you from being fully present during class.

Third, try to find a position at your desk that's physically comfortable. Even if you aren't thinking about how a chair is hurting your back, you still have energy going into that pain and trying to relieve it. Find a comfortable sitting position so that you can focus on the class.

Fourth, take notes in ways that feel good to you, whether that's with a notebook, laptop, or tablet. Finally, be aware of your thoughts while walking into class. Try to keep them positive. By keeping your mind clear of distractions, you'll greatly increase your chances of remembering what you're taught.

[76]
GETTING
GOOD GRADES

Getting good grades usually happens when students attend class regularly, listen to the teacher, take good notes, study hard, and train themselves to take tests calmly.

Attending class is necessary for you to learn the information you need and earn a good grade. While in class, be sure to listen well. This means giving the teacher your fullest attention. Getting enough sleep the night before will also allow you to focus on learning.

While in class, take notes that make sense to you. No one else needs to be able to read and benefit from your notes. As long as they trigger your brain to remember information, then the notes are good. It's also helpful to be in a study group and listen to other explain their understanding of what the teacher taught.

Studying outside the classroom is important too. Find ways to study that work for you. It might be studying in short chunks of time, in a certain room, or at a certain time of day. Find the best pattern for you so that your brain can fully absorb the information When it comes time to taking a test, speak only positive words and thoughts to yourself. Push aside negative thoughts and do you best.

[77]
SPEAKING CONFIDENTLY

As you go through school, you may be called upon to speak in front of your study group, your class, or the whole student body This can be a hard thing to do, and you might feel nervous or unsure. But speaking well is a skill you can learn. Preparing the information you're going to say beforehand will go a long way in calming down your nerves and giving you confidence.

Also, keep in mind that only you know what you intended to say so there's no need to feel embarrassed if your words don't come out perfectly. Only you know if you veered off the script you prepared.

Make sure you stand up straight and take several deep breaths as you walk to the front of the room. This will calm you down. If you feel nervous, you can take several pauses in between your main points. This will keep you from rambling on or speaking so fast that no one can keep up with what you're saying.

Make eye contact with people in the audience, whether it's a study group of five people or a whole room. Eye contact communicates confidence. If you lose track of where you are in speaking your thoughts, take a pause and look down at your notes. Then continue as if nothing happened. If you act like you're confident and in control, most of the time, people will believe that you are.

[78]
COPING WITH LOSSES

In most competitions, there can only be a handful of winners, so it is possible that you could go home from the contest without winning, but you won't be the only one; most entrants in a competition go home without winning.

Will you be disappointed if you don't win? Of course! But is it the end of the world? Absolutely not! It was just rehearsal for your many other future opportunities. Remember, life will offer you plenty of chances to succeed. This was just one of them. By framing losses as learning experiences, you're able to remain resilient and not let it hold you back.

It can feel very discouraging to try our best but not get the result we want. Here is the thing that no one tells you, though: everyone feels that way sometimes. Instead of being discouraged, take a moment to breathe and be proud of yourself for trying something you were afraid to do and use that as motivation to keep trying!

[79]
COMPLETING YOUR HOMEWORK, HONESTLY

Homework is something you'll need to work on for many years, so let's look at ways you can do it quickly and honestly.

Depending on the type of homework, the answers may be immediately available online with just a simple internet search. There are also ways to see the process for reaching the answers, particularly in math. If you have a sports practice that ran late and you're tired, or the family outing to dinner took longer than planned, you may be tempted to just cheat a little by looking up some of the answers online.

Before you do this, stop yourself from thinking those thoughts. It only takes one time of cheating to lead to many more. Instead, if lack of time is the reason you want to be dishonest, tell yourself you'll do homework for 20 minutes and then take a break. Spend those 20 minutes working as hard as you can, and you'll be surprised by how much you can finish.

If being tired is the reason you want to cheat, then do some stretches or squats to get your brain awake before starting. If appropriate, you can even do your homework while standing up at the tall counter in your kitchen. Pushing through the tough moments is the best way to guarantee you learn the material and do well on test days.

[80]
AVOIDING
PLAGIARISM

Plagiarism is when you take the words of someone else and write them, speak them, or type them as if they're your own. This is basically stealing someone else's work. They put time and effort into coming up with specific words or formulas on the topic. Submitting work that you copied from someone else is unfair to them and can get you into big trouble.

When you first are learning how to write a scholarly paper at school, you're told to have verified sources to show that you did your research. This is also to ensure that the opinions of the paper aren't just your own but are also supported by experts. Let's learn how you can do this without copying someone.

First, never use a direct quote unless it's correctly cited. Second, keep in mind that some concepts or facts are commonly known, such as stating that the first president of the United States was named George Washington. You don't have to give credit in those cases.

However, if you find a concept that isn't common knowledge but you don't want to quote it, you can paraphrase it and still give credit to someone else. If you find many concepts that you yourself interpret into something new, that new concept is yours. You don't have to include a source for it. When in doubt, provide your source.

WORKING OUTSIDE SAFELY

[81]
HOW TO
WASH A CAR

One of your chores may be to wash the family car or even you own car. It might sound like a boring job, but washing a car can b a lot of fun. Keep in mind that you'll need certain tools to be abl to wash a car properly.

You'll need a bucket, a sponge, car-washing fluid, paper towels and microfiber cloths. You'll also need a hose or water source First, make sure the car is outside, turned off, and that the alarm isn't activated. Then fill the bucket with water and put soap in it Make sure you don't use household detergent or ordinary soap Only use soap specifically designed for use on a car. Pour in a much as the instructions say, and then place your sponge in the soapy water.

Most people will hose their car down first to remove surface dus and soften things like bird droppings or sap. Then take the sponge and start at the front of the vehicle, wiping down every inch o metal on the car. Work your way to the back of the vehicle, rinsing out your sponge often.

Next, spray your car down to wash off the soap. On the windshield, make sure to use washing fluid and then dry it with paper towels to avoid streaks. You can dry the rest of the car with a cloth. Be sure to rinse out the bucket and the sponge so tha they're ready for the next time.

[82]
PERFORMING
BASIC MAINTENANCE
ON A CAR

Cars are machines that need to be taken care of to run at their very best. Part of this maintenance includes refilling the windshield wiper fluid, checking air in the tires, and checking the oil.

With the help of your parent or another adult, lift the hood of the car. This will reveal the car's engine. Upon closer inspection, you'll see a symbol with windshield wipers on it. Usually, this is at the end of a tube or hose in the engine. After you open this cap, you can pour fluid in so that you have enough to spray on your windshield when you need it.

Most cars will also let you know if the air is low in your tires. To check how low, you can unscrew the plastic caps on each of your tires and use a thin metal gauge to let you know how low the air is. You'll put the end of the gauge into the metal that sticks out of your tire and see if the pressure is okay. Typically, a pressure of 30 or 32 psi is normal.

Finally, you can open the oil cap in your engine and pull out a long rod that will tell you if the oil levels are good or if you need an oil change. These tasks will help your car run well for a long time.

[83]
STAYING SAFE
AROUND VEHICLES

Playing outside is fun and great exercise, but it can also mean that you're near a street or driveway with vehicles. Here are some ways you can enjoy being outside while staying safe.

First, don't play on the part of your driveway that's close to the street. People will often make last-minute decisions to use a stranger's driveway to turn around if they're lost. They may not be paying attention, so it's safer to play near your garage than near the street.

Second, you should be aware of how many cars are around you if you're running or skating. If you're in a parking lot, never run out from your car and into the main drive of the lot. People are often so focused on finding a spot to park in that they may not be looking for people to come out from between parked cars.

Go slow, don't run, and check both ways before you walk from behind your car. Be aware of cars in front of you, beside you, and even behind you for optimum safety. Drivers do their best, but pedestrians need to be very watchful just in case they weren't seen by a driver.

[84]
HOW TO
MOW A LAWN

It's an exciting time when you're old enough to start operating the machines you've probably seen your parents, guardians, or neighbors use. One of these machines is a lawn mower.

Before you start, it's a good idea to wear your oldest sneakers, tuck the laces in, wear long socks or long pants, and put on sunglasses to protect your eyes from any debris. Make sure the gas tank is full and that you know how to turn the machine on and off.

Look at your lawn and see the path you want to make through the grass. Usually, you want to mow straight lines that are orderly and not a zig-zag pattern that will cause you to miss some spots. Be sure an adult is supervising the first few times just in case something goes wrong.

Turn the machine on and prepare to start pushing the lawn mower. Push it at a steady pace, and be aware of any small animals in the grass or any sticks. If you encounter either one, stop the machine, remove the animals or sticks, and then keep going. Not all mowers have bags, but if yours does, then empty the bag of grass when you're finished.

[85]
HANDLING ENGINE OIL OR ANTIFREEZE

Have you ever stood outside while someone was pumping gasoline? You may have noticed a very strong, nasty smell. Strong smells like that often mean that the liquid is toxic and can burn human skin or cause harm if you get too close.

The same is true for other liquids that are essential to making sure our cars are working well. Substances like oil and antifreeze keep the engine going and make sure the brakes don't freeze up on us, but they shouldn't be handled without gloves and eye protection. Never rub your ears, eyes, mouth, or nose after handling chemicals.

If you're learning how to properly use these substances in a car, ask for work gloves. These are thicker and stronger than gardening or winter gloves. They're designed to keep liquids off your hands.

You'll also need to ask for thick, clear eye protection. These are different from reading glasses or sunglasses. They're made to keep your eyes safe and protect your eyes from all angles. If you spill engine oil or antifreeze on yourself, immediately rinse it off and then wash your skin with soap and water.

You don't usually need to add oil and antifreeze on a regular basis, so it can be easy to forget these safety rules. Be sure to follow these rules each time so that you aren't in harm's way.

[86]
IDENTIFYING
VENOMOUS SNAKES

We share this planet with many animals, including snakes. It's vital to know how to tell if a snake is venomous or not. A venomous snake is one that can insert poison into anyone or anything that it bites. This poison can cause great harm or death, depending on the type of snake. Other snakes that are not venomous can still use their fangs to bite, but they don't insert poison into their victim.

If a snake is venomous, it will usually have a triangular-shaped head instead of a round or oval one. Many venomous snakes will have a pointed snout or nose that is tilted up to the sky with pits underneath its nostrils. Hopefully, you never get close enough to look directly into a snake's eyes, but if you do, venomous snakes have vertical pupils in their eyes like cats. Humans have round pupils, and nonvenomous snakes do as well.

Most venomous snakes will also have a thick body to allow them to digest larger prey after they've poisoned them, but this isn't always the case.

If you see a snake of any kind, it's wise to back away slowly and not approach it. Even snakes that aren't venomous can still bite, so it's best to give them their space when out in the wild.

[87]
IDENTIFYING
POISON IVY\OAK

As you take walks or hikes, you'll notice a large number of plants, trees, and bushes. Most of these won't cause you harm, but two can leave large rashes on your skin if you touch their leaves: poison ivy and poison oak.

If you touch the leaves of these plants, your skin will break out into a very itchy, painful rash. This is caused by oil in the leaves that are toxic to human skin. Very sensitive skin can even develop red bumps that are tender to the touch. The rash will usually go away in a few days or less, but if you have concerns, seek medical help immediately.

It's best to avoid both poison ivy and poison oak as much a possible. Many public parks have already removed these from their hiking paths, but be on the lookout just in case. Poison ivy leaves are usually oval with a tip at the end. However, the difference is that they grow in clumps of three from the main vine where other leaves will grow one by one.

The leaves can be lighter green in color and blend in easily with surrounding leaves and foliage. Poison oak leaves look like oak tree leaves due to their darker green color and pointy edge shape, but they grow on a vine instead of an oak tree. If you accidentally touch a leaf, try very hard not to rub at the itchy area. Don't touch your eyes, nose, mouth, or ears at all until you have washed your hands thoroughly.

[88]
STAYING SAFE
DURING BAD WEATHER

Heavy rain with strong winds or a tornado are both scary situations, but there are things you can do to make sure you're as safe as possible. First, remind yourself that you can make wise decisions even if you're scared. Telling yourself soothing things in your mind will help keep you calm.

Second, look at where you're located. If you are in a building like a school, house, or apartment, stay away from the windows. If you can, go down quickly to the ground floor and move toward the center of the building, away from doors and windows. When a tornado happens, sometimes big objects like picnic tables, bicycles, and even BBQ grills can be pushed against windows or doors, harming anyone who is nearby.

If you and your family are in a car when a tornado or storm comes into the area, be sure to pull over and seek shelter in a building as quickly as possible. It isn't wise to remain in a vehicle during a tornado because of the strong winds. Be sure to stay with your guardians, or if you are with school peers, stay near a trusted adult and follow their instructions. Panicking and going out on your own isn't a good idea. You'll only put yourself in harm's way.

[89]
USING A RADIO
FOR EMERGENCIES

Check with your caregivers or parents to see if they have what's called an emergency radio. An emergency radio acts like a phone that you can use to listen to emergency broadcasts during disasters such as earthquakes, tornadoes, floods, and other sudden storms. Some of the smaller radios can even look like walkie-talkies, making them very easy to grab and bring with you.

If you need to leave during an emergency or you go hiking, camping, or out on a boat, then an emergency radio is good to have with you. These radios usually operate on batteries and can be connected to a generator. If an emergency is happening, some radios have an orange button that you can use to send an SOS signal.

An SOS signal communicates that you're in danger and need help. This button on the radio should only be used in absolute danger. Talk to your family to learn how to set the dial on the front of the radio to the correct frequency for your area. A frequency is displayed as numbers around the dial. Each number will send your message to a different radio location, so be sure to know which numbers you can use in an emergency.

[90]
READING A
MAP

Maps have varying levels of detail, but many types show basic geographical features like rivers, hills, mountains, and roads. You can usually see the names of large cities as well as smaller towns. Maps will also have lines that run up and down and left to right. These are grid lines that help you know the direction you're going.

The most important part of reading a map is knowing where you are on the map. Most people will mark where their starting point is, whether that's your home or your campground, if you're using the map to go for a hike. The second most important thing to know is where you want to end up. You can mark this on the map too. Then you'll need to see where north, south, east, and west are in relation to your location. You can figure this out by using a compass or by looking at the sky.

The sun rises each morning in the east and sets each night in the west. A compass rose marked on the map will show you the cardinal directions. Turn your body until the map lines up with where you are and what's around you. Then carefully begin to trek from your starting point to your destination, turning the map to keep it oriented correctly as you walk.

[91]
SAFELY ASK
FOR DIRECTIONS

Hopefully, you never find yourself alone in public or separated from your friends, school group, or family. But if you do, it's understandable to feel scared and not know what to do.

Before you do anything else, take a couple of deep breaths. Try your phone to see if you can call someone you trust for help. If you don't have your phone with you, you may need to ask for directions so that you can walk back to the area you last saw your group in. It's always a good idea to have a meeting place planned out during an outing. That way, everyone knows to immediately go to that area if you're separated.

The first step in asking for directions is to do so in a public place with many people around. Don't give any personal information to a stranger who approaches you asking if you're lost. Instead, tell the person no and walk to a store or business that has customers in it. Ask one of the staff who's working there if they can point you in the direction of your meeting place or put out an alert over the intercom to page your group.

Don't accept a ride in a stranger's car or allow them to walk with you if you know the way once they give you directions. Run immediately if they attempt to take your arm or walk you in a different direction than where you need to go. Trust yourself and keep your distance from strangers until you're reunited with your group.

MAINTAINING
YOUR APPEARANCE

[92]
CARING FOR
YOUR HAIR

Hair comes in so many colors and textures, but regardless of what kind of hair you have, you need to take care of it. Some people like their hair to be short, while others like for it to be long. Depending on what type of hair you have, how you care for it will be special and unique to you.

Taking care of your hair means knowing how often you should wash it, how you should let it dry if you should brush or comb it, or if there's another method to detangle it. Hair can have a wide variety of qualities. All hair is beautiful and worth putting the time in to keep it looking healthy.

It's important not to compare your hair to anyone else's. You may need to use two different gels or mousses on your hair, while your friend doesn't need as much product. Knowing how to wash, condition, brush, and style your own hair is the only thing you should be focusing on.

[93]
STYLING YOUR
HAIR

Styling your hair is a learned skill that will take time and practice, but you can get there! If someone has styled your hair in a way you like, carefully watch the next time they do it and remember those techniques. You can even ask them to teach you a style that you like.

Many styles have a few steps to them. You may need to learn how to part or adjust your hair before applying product. You may need to learn how to finger-curl your hair or scrunch it. Knowing each of these steps will help you feel confident. If there are hot tools involved, such as a hair dryer, curling iron, or straightener, make sure you know how to use them to avoid damaging your hair. Only use them for the first time if someone is watching, and make sure you don't accidentally burn yourself.

You may even want to have someone else do your hair on a regular basis. In that case, you should choose which type of hairstyle you want and know how to communicate that to a professional. You may also need to pretreat your hair before your appointment or learn about how to care for your hairstyle. For example, you might need to ask your stylist about protecting your curls in bad weather or the best way to wash your new box braids before you leave.

As you learn more ways to style your hair, you can really show your personality and feel confident in the way you look.

[94]
MAKING TIME
TO PLAN OUTFITS

If you're a busy young person, you might have school clubs, sports, music groups, or religious activities on top of your homework, family time, and time with friends. It can feel like a lot of work to choose the right outfits for different situations. Some students have a uniform for school, so there may not be a lot of choices when you choose your clothing.

Let's talk about how to choose your clothes for any occasion. It's a good idea to learn this skill now. As you get older and start your first job or go on a first date, you'll want to know how to put together an outfit.

First, choose clean clothes. Second, choose colors that aren't too similar to each other. You may not want to wear a red shirt and pink shorts. Usually, you'll wear brown, black, or blue jeans as pants or shorts and a shirt that's either fancy or casual, depending on the day. Planning your outfits before you go out of the house will help you look appropriate for the occasion while also showing others that you respect yourself and you're looking forward to whatever you have planned.

Wearing something that's too casual or wrinkled, for example, may communicate that you're sloppy or not good with details. You can avoid this by planning beforehand.

[95]
TAKING CARE
OF YOUR SKIN

t's amazing to think about how many different places there are to ive in this world. Some places are very hot, while others are cold. Some are humid, and others are dry. Weather plays a big role in how you take care of your skin!

Take a moment to think about the weather where you live. After you take a shower, you may need to put lotion on your skin because the weather may be dry or cold. You don't want your skin to look scaly or to crack. If it's hot out, you may not put a lot of lotion on because it could cause you to sweat even more when you're outside.

The biggest thing to remember when taking care of your skin is to keep it clean and use the right type and amount of lotion. It's a good idea to research the ingredients in your skincare products to make sure they're appropriate for you. For example, fragrances and harsh chemicals can damage sensitive skin. Understanding your skin's needs will help you take care of it for the rest of your life, long after you grow up and begin your adult life.

[96]
APPLYING
SPF PROTECTION

Have you ever heard about SPF? SPF means *sun protection factor* and it's a fancy way of measuring how much protection a particular sunscreen provides from the sun. This protection i measured through numbers. For example, a sunscreen may have an SPF of 35 or even 70. The bigger the number, the more protection you can expect to receive from the sun.

Some sun exposure is completely normal and healthy, but staying in the sun for hours on end without protection can cause your skin to burn. You can apply sunscreen either as a lotion or a spray. I might be annoying when your parent calls you over in the middle of an activity to tell you to put on sunscreen, but they're doing that for good reason. As you play, swim, or sweat in the sun, the sunscreen may wipe or wash off, so putting more on every hour i normal and will keep your skin safe.

Be sure to cover your skin thoroughly. Don't rush or skip over any spots that are hard to reach. Give it a few minutes to dry before you head back into the pool or outside to play again.

[97]
ADHERING TO
A DRESS CODE

A dress code is a set of rules for what each person can wear. Usually, you'll find that schools have very clear dress codes. People in charge have thought through how they want the students to dress so that everyone looks similar, and the focus can be on learning new things. Dress codes also are in place at work, which you'll discover when you're older. Let's discuss how to understand more about these rules.

First, take the time to read the dress code. Then ask your teachers, guardians, or parents about anything you don't understand. Ask them to help you put clothes from your closet in a separate section if they adhere to the dress code. This way, you know which clothes you can wear for which occasions. Then you can plan your outfits for school or wherever the dress code is in place. Try not to grumble about having a dress code. Instead, focus on the clothes you *can* wear. Try to be happy that outside of school, you can probably wear whatever you want from your closet.

It might be helpful to choose a few of your favorite items from the dress code section of your closet to wear if you're feeling disappointed about the dress code. Remember that you can still look cute even when following the dress code!

[98]
IRONING
YOUR CLOTHES

Doing laundry is often a chore that takes a long time. Maybe you forgot to move the clothes from the washer to the dryer or from the dryer to the closet, where they need to be either hung up or folded. If clothing stays too long in a clean pile in a basket or too long in the dryer, they will get wrinkles on them.

This is okay if it's your pajamas, but most times, it isn't okay to wear something wrinkled to school or a function like a birthday party. You may need to use an ironing board and an iron. Make sure you have help from an adult if you've never handled an iron before.

To iron your clothes, you need to open the ironing board and set it up. Then you need to plug in the iron and set it upright with the metal part off the ironing board. The metal part of the iron is designed to get hot so that it can press down on the wrinkles and get rid of them. You'll want to do this by pressing very carefully and avoiding buttons and zippers as you slowly move the iron across the fabric.

Always turn off and then unplug the iron when you're done before you walk away. Let the iron cool off completely after it's turned off, and then put it away.

[99]
FINDING YOUR
OWN STYLE

Have you ever looked at a friend, an older sibling or cousin, or someone on TV and thought about how much you would like to have the outfit they're wearing because it looked so good on them? For most of us, this will happen often. It's part of building your own sense of style.

A style is a certain type of clothing or color combination that a person likes to wear. Styles can be defined as casual, sporty, chic, athletic, preppy, and more. As you grow up, it will be normal for you to try out many different types.

Regardless of your style, make sure you show appreciation for the clothing that your parents or caregivers buy for you, and let them know if you're experimenting with a few different trends. You may need to describe the style you like to help others understand.

If you can, try clothes on in a store and see how you feel in them. If you don't like an item, ask yourself what exactly about it you don't like before just rejecting it. It might be the color, the size, or the texture of the fabric more than the style itself.

It's also a good idea to note what style you think looks good on your body. Certain styles might look good on someone else, but when you put them on yourself, you may decide it doesn't look the way you hoped it would.

This is completely normal and has nothing to do with how your body looks. It's about the clothes themselves. You never need to change your body to fit into a brand or type of clothing.

[100]
BRUSHING AND
FLOSSING YOUR
TEETH

You probably already know how important it is to brush your teeth. Your parents and grandparents may have told you this, and your dentist has definitely told you so. It might seem like a waste of time to brush your teeth every single day, and especially twice a day, but having a cavity filled will help you understand why it's so important.

Teeth can sometimes decay, and it isn't fun to get a filling. When you don't brush, food can get stuck in tiny places between your teeth. This food will become acidic as it breaks down in your mouth, and that acidity can start to create a little hole in your tooth.

Eventually, this hole will become bigger and bigger if other food gets stuck in the same spot. Over time, your dentist will discover the hole and will need to put a filling in it. This means that the dentist will drill the hole a little bit so that the filling can be pushed into the hole. Usually, the drilling part can hurt a little bit. It's a very good idea to brush and floss your teeth to avoid needing a filling.

To brush your teeth, you need a clean toothbrush. Squeeze toothpaste on your toothbrush and start on one side of your mouth, brushing with care all along the inside and outside of that row of teeth. Then move to the other row of teeth. If you have an electric toothbrush, then you can let that do most of the work. You'll need to brush for three minutes total to make sure you've removed the food from your teeth. Ask your dentist if they want you to floss before or after you brush.

[101]
LIKING THE
WAY YOU LOOK

Each of us looks a little different from every other person. Even in families, siblings can look very different. Sometimes, a trend in school or on TV can glorify the way one particular person looks and makes the rest of us feel like we're not good enough because we don't look like that person. It's a good idea to learn how to compliment others for their unique look while also celebrating and complimenting yourself.

Try to look at yourself in the mirror every day and find three things you love about how your appearance. It's so important that we learn to feel confident in who we are and to always think nice thoughts about ourselves. If you start wishing you looked like someone else; you should try and stop those thoughts. Instead, think about the things you're proud of or things about yourself that make you so different from everyone else. If you learn to be your own cheerleader, nothing in life will be able to keep you down.

CONCLUSION

As we reflect on the topics in this book, it's important to remember that these are only starting points to learning about life. As you get older, you'll undergo many changes and improve on most of these skills naturally. To get better at anything, though, it is important you make time to practice. Asking your friends, family, and neighbors to help or join you is an excellent way to get real-life experience with these life lessons. Learning how to do our laundry, putting together an outfit that helps us feel confident, or navigating healthy relationships are tasks that will take time to master. Now that you've read through the whole book feel free to look up additional resources. You can find books at your library, ask a parent or guardian, or even research online, with an adult, to further your understanding of these topics. Don't be discouraged if you feel like you mess up sometimes or are not good at something; it's all part of the process of growing up! Keeping a positive attitude and a commitment to growth will help you master everything in this book in no time!

Made in the USA
Las Vegas, NV
30 October 2023

79854694R00075